# COOKING METHODS FOR BEGINNERS

# NO-BAKE DESSERTS

Maryah Silvestri

# Table of Contents

# PUDDING PIE
# RECIPES

# Homemade Banana Pudding Pie

Serving: 8 | Prep: 30m | Ready in: 2h

## Ingredients

• 2 cups vanilla wafer crumbs

• 3 bananas, sliced into 1/4 inch slices

• 1 1/2 cups white sugar

• 1/4 cup all-purpose flour

• 2 cups milk

• 3 egg yolks

• 2 teaspoons butter

• 2 teaspoons vanilla extract

• 3 egg whites

• 1/4 cup white sugar

## Direction

• Set oven to 350°F (175°C) to preheat.

• Fill the bottom and sides of a 9-inch pie plate with 1 layer of alternating vanilla wafer crumbs and banana slices.

• Prepare Pudding: Mix flour with 1 1/2 cups sugar in a medium saucepan. Stir well, then mix in 1/2 the milk. Whisk egg yolks and stir into sugar mixture. Put in butter or margarine and remaining milk.

• Over low heat, cook mixture until thickened, mixing constantly. Take off from heat and mix in vanilla extract. Put 1/2 of pudding on vanilla wafer and banana layer while it's still hot.

• Prepare another layer of alternating vanilla wafers and banana slices over pudding layer. Put remaining pudding on top of the second wafer and banana layer.

• Prepare Meringue: Whisk egg whites until foamy in a large glass or metal bowl. Put in 1/4 cup sugar little by little, keep mixing until whites turn stiff. Put meringue evenly into pie pan, be sure to cover pudding layer completely.

• Bake for 15 minutes in preheated oven, just until meringue is browned. Refrigerate before serving.

**Nutrition Information**

• Calories: 504 calories;
• Total Carbohydrate: 92.1 g

• Cholesterol: 84 mg

• Total Fat: 12.8 g

• Protein: 7.2 g

• Sodium: 194 mg

# Jimmy Carter Dessert

Serving: 16

## Ingredients

- 1 1/2 cups graham cracker crumbs
- 1/4 cup white sugar
- 1/3 cup butter, melted
- 1 (8 ounce) package cream cheese
- 1/3 cup peanut butter
- 2 (8 ounce) containers frozen whipped topping, thawed
- 1 cup confectioners' sugar
- 1 (3.4 ounce) package instant vanilla pudding mix
- 1 (3.9 ounce) package instant chocolate pudding mix
- 3 cups milk
- 1/4 cup chopped peanuts
- 1/8 cup grated semisweet chocolate

## Direction

• Combine melted butter or margarine, sugar, and graham cracker crumbs. Firmly press into a 13 x 9-inch pan's bottom.

• Beat together peanut butter and the cream cheese until smooth. Stir the confectioners' sugar and 2 cups of the whipped topping in. Layer mixture over the crust.

• Combine milk and the pudding mixes, and layer on top the peanut butter. Spread the reserved whipped topping on top. Sprinkle shaved chocolate and chopped peanuts on top. Refrigerate.

## Nutrition Information

• Calories: 368 calories;
• Total Carbohydrate: 39.4 g

• Cholesterol: 29 mg

• Total Fat: 21.9 g

• Protein: 5.6 g

• Sodium: 350 mg

# Julie's Pistachio Delight

Serving: 16

## Ingredients

• 4 cups milk

• 2 (3 ounce) packages instant pistachio pudding mix

• 1 (8 ounce) can pineapple tidbits, drained

• 1 cup chopped walnuts

• 1 cup mini marshmallows

• 1/2 cup shredded coconut

• 2 (9 inch) prepared graham cracker crusts

## Direction

• In a large bowl, whisk pudding mix and milk together. Refrigerate about 1 hour until firm. Mix coconut, marshmallows, walnuts and pineapple tidbits into pudding. Put pudding mixture evenly into the prepped graham cracker crusts.

## Nutrition Information

- Calories: 305 calories;
- Total Carbohydrate: 40.6 g

- Cholesterol: 5 mg

- Total Fat: 14.3 g

- Protein: 4.5 g

- Sodium: 383 mg

# Pluot And Star Fruit French Vanilla Pudding Pie

Serving: 8 | Prep: 15m | Ready in: 35m

## Ingredients

• 1 (9 inch) prepared pie crust

• 2 cups milk

• 1 (3.5 ounce) package instant French vanilla pudding mix

• 1 star fruit

• 3 pluots, halved and pitted

## Direction

• Heat oven to 400°F (205°C). Put the pie shell into a 9 inches pie pan.

• In the heated oven, bake the pie shell about 10 minutes or until golden brown. Put aside to rest.

• In a large bowl, whip together the instant pudding and milk; put aside. Cut 5 attractive, thin, star-shaped pieces from the center of the star fruit, and save for later use. Slice the rest of the star fruit finely. Slice and save 10 attractive, thin, half-moon-shaped slices of a pluot, and save for later use; slice the rest of the pluots finely. Combine chopped fruit into the pudding. Put the pudding mixture into the prepared pie shell; chill about 10 minutes until firm.

• Put the saved pieces of star fruit and pluot on top of the pie, serve.

## Nutrition Information

• Calories: 205 calories;
• Total Carbohydrate: 28.3 g

• Cholesterol: 5 mg

• Total Fat: 8.8 g

• Protein: 3.7 g

• Sodium: 319 mg

# Pumpkin Chiffon Pie Ii

Serving: 8 | Prep: 30m | Ready in: 4h

## Ingredients

• 2 3/4 cups nonfat milk

• 2 (1.5 ounce) envelopes sugar-free instant vanilla pudding mix

• 1 (15 ounce) can pumpkin puree

• 1 teaspoon ground cinnamon

• 1/2 teaspoon ground ginger

• 1/4 teaspoon ground cloves

• 1 (9 inch) reduced fat graham cracker pie crust

## Direction

• Mix the pudding mix and milk in a large mixing bowl. Blend for 1 minute with electric beaters. Put in cloves, ginger, cinnamon and pumpkin and blend for 1 more minute. Put filling into the prepared crust. Wrap it up and chill until firm or for 2 hours.

## Nutrition Information

• Calories: 173 calories;

• Total Carbohydrate: 31 g

• Cholesterol: 2 mg

• Total Fat: 3.8 g

• Protein: 4.5 g

• Sodium: 685 mg

# Pumpkin Pudding Pie

Serving: 8 | Prep: 20m | Ready in: 1h27m

## Ingredients

• Crust:

• 1 1/2 cups graham cracker crumbs

• 6 tablespoons butter, melted

• 1/3 cup white sugar

• 1/4 teaspoon pumpkin pie spice

• Filling:

• 1 (5.1 ounce) package instant vanilla pudding mix

• 1 (12 fluid ounce) can 2% evaporated milk

• 1 (15 ounce) can pumpkin puree

• 3/4 teaspoon pumpkin pie spice

## Direction

• To preheat: Set oven to 190°C (375°F).

• Put 1/4 teaspoon pumpkin pie spice, white sugar, butter, and graham cracker crumbs together in a bowl then stir; press into the bottom and up the sides of a 9-inch pie dish.

• Put the dish in the preheated oven then bake for about 7 minutes till crust turns lightly brown. Let pie crust cool completely.

• Put evaporated milk and pudding mix together in a bowl then whisk bowl for 2 minutes. Keep pudding in the fridge to allow it to chill for 5 minutes. Stir 3/4 teaspoon pumpkin pie spice and pumpkin into pudding till everything is mixed well. Use pudding filling to spread into cooled pie crust then keep in the fridge for about half an hour until it is chilled.

## Nutrition Information

• Calories: 323 calories;
• Total Carbohydrate: 46.2 g

• Cholesterol: 37 mg

• Total Fat: 14.1 g

• Protein: 5 g

# Quick And Easy Chocolate Pie

Serving: 8 | Ready in: 6h15m

## Ingredients

• 1 (12 ounce) can evaporated milk

• 1 (5.9 ounce) package chocolate instant pudding mix

• 1 (6.5 ounce) can Reddi-wip® Original Dairy Whipped Topping

• 1/2 cup miniature semi-sweet chocolate morsels (optional)

• 1 (9 inch) graham cracker pie crust

• Additional Reddi-wip Original Whipped Light Cream and crushed candy (optional)

## Direction

• In a medium bowl, pour milk then add dry pudding mix; use a wire whisk to beat till everything is well blended and the mixture just begins becoming thick. Add chocolate morsels in and stir, according to your preference.

• Put in contents of Reddi-wip can; stir with care but quickly till well blended. Transfer mixture into crust; put a lid on.

• Keep in the fridge for 6 hours or till it is set. Slice into 8 pieces to serve. Use crushed candy and extra Reddi-wip to garnish according to your liking.

**Nutrition Information**

• Calories: 404 calories;
• Total Carbohydrate: 53.4 g

• Cholesterol: 36 mg

• Total Fat: 19 g

• Protein: 5.1 g

• Sodium: 512 mg

# Quick And Easy Lemon Pie

Serving: 8 | Prep: 15m | Ready in: 2h15m

## Ingredients

- 1 (4.3 ounce) package non-instant lemon pudding mix
- 1 (8 ounce) package cream cheese
- 1/2 (14 ounce) can sweetened condensed milk
- 3 tablespoons lemon juice
- 1 (9 inch) prepared graham cracker crust
- 1 (8 ounce) container frozen whipped topping, thawed

## Direction

- Prepare pudding following package directions. When pudding thickens, reduce heat to low. Mix in lemon juice, condensed milk, and cream cheese. Mix often because mixture may stick to the pan.
- Put mixture into graham cracker shell. Cover and chill in the fridge. Serve with whipped topping when ready.

## Nutrition Information

- Calories: 458 calories;
- Total Carbohydrate: 53.3 g

- Cholesterol: 39 mg

- Total Fat: 24 g

- Protein: 5.3 g

- Sodium: 361 mg

# Krissy's Easy Chocolate Triple Layer Pie

Serving: 8 | Prep: 10m | Ready in: 4h10m

## Ingredients

- 2 cups cold milk
- 2 (3.9 ounce) packages instant chocolate pudding mix
- 1 (9 inch) prepared graham cracker crust, chocolate
- 1 (8 ounce) container frozen whipped topping, thawed
- 1/2 cup chocolate shavings

## Direction

- Mix pudding and milk in a large bowl. Whisk for 1 minute using wire whisk. Into a graham cracker crust, scoop in 1 1/2 cups of pudding.
- Fold gently 1/2 of the whipped topping into the remaining pudding. Spread it over the pudding on top of the crust. Layer the other half of the whipped topping on

top. Sprinkle with shaved chocolate, cover and refrigerate for 4 hours.

## Nutrition Information

- Calories: 422 calories;
- Total Carbohydrate: 55 g

- Cholesterol: 8 mg

- Total Fat: 20.7 g

- Protein: 5.3 g

- Sodium: 618 mg

# Passover Chocolate Mousse Pie

Serving: 8

## Ingredients

- 10 kosher for Passover chocolate wafers
- 1 tablespoon butter, melted
- 6 ounces semi-sweet chocolate chips
- 1/4 cup water
- 1/4 cup white sugar
- 2 eggs
- 1 (7 ounce) can whipped cream

## Direction

- In a medium-size mixing bowl, crush the chocolate wafers. Mix the melted butter or margarine with the chocolate crumbs. Push mixture into a 9 inches pie plan with your hands.

• In the top of a double boiler, melt chocolate chips. Mix sometimes until silky. Put water into the chocolate and continue mixing until combined. Take the chocolate away from the heat.

• Whisk the eggs and sugar until thick and light in color. Fold the chocolate mixture into the bowl with the eggs and sugar. Fold half of the whipped cream into the mixture. Spread mixture into the pie shell. Garnish with remaining cream.

## Nutrition Information

• Calories: 276 calories;
• Total Carbohydrate: 31.9 g

• Cholesterol: 73 mg

• Total Fat: 15.7 g

• Protein: 4.7 g

• Sodium: 60 mg

# Pastry Cream For Pies

Serving: 8 | Prep: 30m | Ready in: 1h

## Ingredients

- 1 cup milk
- 3 egg yolks
- 1/2 cup white sugar
- 1/4 cup all-purpose flour
- 1 tablespoon butter
- 1 tablespoon vanilla extract

## Direction

- Heat milk to boiling point in a small saucepan, then take off heat.
- Beat egg yolks in a heatproof mixing bowl until smooth. Add the granulated sugar in slowly and keep on beating until it becomes pale yellow. Mix the flour in.

- Steadily stream hot milk into the egg yolk mixture, beating continuously. When finish adding the milk, put the bowl on top of (not inside) a pan of boiling water, or put the egg mixture in the top of a double boiler. Heat and stir continuously, until it thickens. Cook for 2 more minutes, then take off heat. Stir in the vanilla and butter. Cover with plastic wrap and let cool.

## Nutrition Information

- Calories: 115 calories;
- Total Carbohydrate: 17.3 g
- Cholesterol: 83 mg
- Total Fat: 3.7 g
- Protein: 2.4 g
- Sodium: 26 mg

# Peanut Butter And Fudge Swirl Pie

Serving: 8 | Prep: 15m | Ready in: 4h15m

## Ingredients

• 1 (8 ounce) package PHILADELPHIA Cream Cheese, softened

• 1/2 cup sugar

• 1/4 cup creamy peanut butter

• 2 cups thawed COOL WHIP Whipped Topping

• 1 (6 ounce) OREO Pie Crust

• 1/4 cup hot fudge ice cream topping, warmed

**Direction**

• In a large bowl, put peanut butter, sugar, cream cheese, then use a mixer to beat until blended. Stir in COOL WHIP gently.

• Spoon into crust; pour drizzles of fudge topping on top. Use a knife to swirl gently.

• Keep in the fridge for 4 hours or until becoming firm. Keep the leftovers in the fridge.

**Nutrition Information**

• Calories: 358 calories;

• Total Carbohydrate: 40.3 g

• Cholesterol: 32 mg

• Total Fat: 21.4 g

• Protein: 4.9 g

• Sodium: 306 mg

# Persimmon Pudding Pie

Serving: 8 | Prep: 15m | Ready in: 1h15m

## Ingredients

- 2 tablespoons butter, melted
- 2 cups persimmon pulp
- 2 cups white sugar
- 3 eggs, lightly beaten
- 1 1/4 cups buttermilk
- 1 teaspoon baking soda
- 2 cups all-purpose flour
- 1 teaspoon baking powder
- 1/2 teaspoon ground cinnamon
- 1/2 teaspoon salt
- 1/2 teaspoon vanilla extract

## Direction

• Heat oven to 165 degrees C or 325 degrees F. Evenly spread dissolved butter on the bottom of a baking dish.

• Beat sugar and persimmon pulp in a bowl. Mix in eggs. Mix in baking soda and buttermilk.

• Sift salt, cinnamon, baking powder, and flour in a bowl. Slowly add flour mixture to the persimmon mixture, mixing until well combined. Mix in vanilla extract. Place persimmon batter in the prepared baking dish.

• Bake in the oven for an hour until cooked through and lightly golden.

## Nutrition Information

• Calories: 451 calories;
• Total Carbohydrate: 95.8 g

• Cholesterol: 79 mg

• Total Fat: 5.6 g

• Protein: 7.4 g

• Sodium: 452 mg

# Pistachio Cream Pie

Serving: 8 | Prep: 25m | Ready in: 1h45m

## Ingredients

- 1 1/2 cups all-purpose flour
- 1/4 cup chopped walnuts
- 3/4 cup butter, softened
- 1 (8 ounce) package cream cheese, softened
- 1 teaspoon vanilla extract
- 1 cup confectioners' sugar
- 1 (16 ounce) container frozen whipped topping, thawed
- 2 (3 ounce) packages instant pistachio pudding mix
- 3 cups cold milk
- 1/4 cup maraschino cherries
- 1/8 cup chopped pistachio nuts

## Direction

• To preheat: Set oven to 175°C (350°F).

• Put butter, walnuts, flour together and mix well. Press the mixture into the bottom of a 9 x 13-inch pan. Put in the preheated oven and bake for 20-30 minutes until you can smell fragrance from the nuts and the crust turns lightly brown. Let it cool.

• Put a cup of whipped topping, confectioners' sugar, vanilla, cream cheese together then mix. Beat well then use the filling to spread on the cooled crust. Keep in the fridge for an hour.

• Put milk and instant pudding together then mix until thick. Arrange the pudding on top of the layer of cream cheese. Then put the remaining whipped topping on top of the pudding; use nuts to sprinkle, and maraschino cherries to decorate.

## Nutrition Information

- Calories: 762 calories;
- Total Carbohydrate: 76.7 g

- Cholesterol: 84 mg

- Total Fat: 47.1 g

- Protein: 9.4 g

- Sodium: 619 mg

# PEANUT BUTTER RECIPES

# Double Layer Chocolate Peanut Butter Pie

Serving: 8 | Prep: 20m | Ready in: 4h20m

## Ingredients

- 1/2 (8 ounce) package cream cheese, softened
- 1 tablespoon white sugar
- 1 tablespoon cold milk
- 1 cup peanut butter
- 1 (8 ounce) container frozen whipped topping, thawed
- 1 (9 inch) prepared graham cracker crust
- 2 (3.9 ounce) packages instant chocolate pudding mix
- 2 cups cold milk
- 4 peanut butter cups, cut into 1/2 inch pieces

## Direction

• Whip peanut butter, 1 tablespoon milk, sugar and cream cheese in a large bowl until smooth. Lightly mix in 1 1/2 cups of whipped topping. Put mixture evenly on bottom of pie crust.

• Mix pudding mix with 2 cups milk in a second bowl until thick. Mix in remaining whipped topping right away. Put mixture evenly over peanut butter layer.

• Sprinkle peanut butter cups on top of pie. Cover and chill for 4 hours.

## Nutrition Information

• Calories: 648 calories;
• Total Carbohydrate: 65.6 g

• Cholesterol: 21 mg

• Total Fat: 37.6 g

• Protein: 14 g

• Sodium: 803 mg

# Ez Peanut Butter Pie I

Serving: 8

## Ingredients

- 1 (8 ounce) package cream cheese, softened
- 1 cup white sugar
- 1 teaspoon vanilla extract
- 2/3 cup creamy peanut butter
- 1 (8 ounce) container frozen whipped topping, thawed
- 1 (9 inch) pie shell, baked

## Direction

- Combine vanilla, sugar and the cream cheese together. Add in the peanut butter and mix until well combined. Fold the dessert topping in until fully blended.
- Fill the peanut butter mixture into the pie crust and put in the freezer until it is ready to serve. Note: Best served with a chocolate crust and chocolate chip sprinkles.

## Nutrition Information

- Calories: 530 calories;
- Total Carbohydrate: 47.2 g

- Cholesterol: 31 mg

- Total Fat: 35.5 g

- Protein: 9.3 g

- Sodium: 311 mg

# Ez Peanut Butter Pie Ii

Serving: 8 | Prep: 10m | Ready in: 20m

## Ingredients

- 1 (9 inch) prepared graham cracker crust
- 1 (4.6 ounce) package non-instant vanilla pudding mix
- 1 cup peanut butter

## Direction

- Prepare, cook and serve the pudding as instructed on package label. Add in peanut butter and stir. Bring mixture to a boil then transfer into graham cracker crust. Let it cool.

## Nutrition Information

- Calories: 398 calories;
- Total Carbohydrate: 40.8 g

- Cholesterol: 0 mg

- Total Fat: 23.8 g

- Protein: 9.4 g

- Sodium: 440 mg

# Fluffy Peanut Butter Pie

Serving: 8 | Prep: 40m | Ready in: 5h10m

## Ingredients

- 1/3 cup butter
- 1 cup semisweet chocolate chips
- 2 1/2 cups crispy rice cereal
- 1 (8 ounce) package cream cheese, softened
- 1 (14 ounce) can sweetened condensed milk
- 3/4 cup peanut butter
- 3 tablespoons lemon juice
- 1 teaspoon vanilla extract
- 1 cup heavy whipping cream, whipped
- 2 teaspoons chocolate syrup

## Direction

• Prepare Crust: Melt chocolate chips and butter in a heavy saucepan over low heat. Take away from heat. Slowly mix in rice cereal until each piece is coated completely.

• Push mixture down into the bottom and up sides of a gently greased 9 inches pie dish. Refrigerate for half an hour.

• Prepare Filling: Whip cream cheese in a large bowl until fluffy. Stir peanut butter and condensed milk into cream cheese until silky. Mix in vanilla and lemon juice, then fold in whipped cream.

• Put mixture into pie shell. Pour syrup slowly on top of pie; lightly swirl with a spoon. Cover and chill pie for 4 hours or until set. Chill leftovers.

## Nutrition Information

• Calories: 707 calories;
• Total Carbohydrate: 55.3 g

• Cholesterol: 109 mg

• Total Fat: 51.3 g

• Protein: 14.3 g

# Light And Fluffy Peanut Butter Pie

Serving: 8 | Prep: 10m | Ready in: 2h10m

## Ingredients

- 1 (9 inch) prepared graham cracker crust
- 1 (16 ounce) jar reduced fat peanut butter
- 1 cup confectioners' sugar
- 1 (8 ounce) package cream cheese, softened

## Direction

- Put cream cheese, confectioners' sugar, and peanut butter together in a medium mixing bowl then mix. Whip until the mixture becomes fluffy and smooth. Transfer mixture into graham cracker crust then allow it to chill for 2 hours before serving.

## Nutrition Information

- Calories: 570 calories;
- Total Carbohydrate: 51 g

- Cholesterol: 31 mg

- Total Fat: 35.1 g

- Protein: 18.7 g

- Sodium: 544 mg

# Mile-high Peanut Butter Pie

Serving: 12 | Prep: 15m | Ready in: 3h40m

## Ingredients

• 35 NILLA Wafers, finely crushed

• 1/4 cup butter, melted

• 1 (3.9 ounce) package JELL-O Chocolate Instant Pudding

• 2 cups cold milk, divided

• 4 ounces PHILADELPHIA Cream Cheese, softened

• 1 (3.4 ounce) package JELL-O Vanilla Flavor Instant Pudding

• 1/2 cup PLANTERS Creamy Peanut Butter, divided

• 2 cups thawed COOL WHIP Whipped Topping, divided

• 1/2 ounce BAKER'S Semi-Sweet Chocolate

## Direction

• Preheat oven to 375°F.

• Stir butter and wafer crumbs until combined; push down to bottom and up sides of 9-inch pie plate. Bake for 10 minutes then cool.

• Whip 1 cup milk and chocolate pudding mix with a whisk for 2 minutes. (Pudding will be thick.) Put onto bottom of crust and evenly spread out. In a large bowl, add remaining milk to cream cheese gradually with mixer until combined. Put in vanilla pudding mix; whip for 2 minutes. Save 1 tablespoon peanut butter. Put remaining to vanilla pudding mixture; whip until combined. Mix in 1 cup cool whip. Put over chocolate pudding layer evenly to within 1 inch of edge. Scoop leftover cool whip onto middle of pie.

• Chill 3 hours. Just before serving, microwave remaining peanut butter in microwave safe bowl on high for 15 seconds or until melted. Melt chocolate following directions on package. Pour chocolate and peanut butter over pie.

## Nutrition Information

- Calories: 287 calories;
- Total Carbohydrate: 31.3 g
- Cholesterol: 26 mg
- Total Fat: 16.3 g
- Protein: 4.8 g
- Sodium: 424 mg

# Mysweetcreations Peanut Butter Cookie Pie

Serving: 8 | Prep: 20m | Ready in: 30m

## Ingredients

• 18 cream-filled chocolate sandwich cookies (such as Oreo®), crushed

• 1 1/2 tablespoons butter

• 1/2 teaspoon ground cinnamon

• 1 (8 ounce) package cream cheese, softened

• 1 cup confectioners' sugar

• 1 teaspoon vanilla extract

• 1 cup creamy peanut butter

• 3 cups frozen whipped topping, thawed

• 3/4 cup frozen whipped topping, thawed

• 2 tablespoons chocolate sundae syrup (such as Smucker's®)

• 2 tablespoons caramel sundae syrup (such as Smucker's®)

• 4 peanut butter cups (such as Reese's®), chopped

## Direction

• Preheat oven to 175°C/350°F. In a bowl, mix cinnamon, butter and chocolate cookies. At the bottom of a springform 9-in. pan, firmly press mixture.
• Bake in preheated oven for 8 minutes till crust harden. Put aside. Cool.

• Beat vanilla extract, confectioners' sugar and cream cheese. Mix peanut butter in till blended well. Fold 3 cups whipped topping in till mixture is fluffy and light. Put mixture onto cooled cookie crust. Evenly spread on top.

• In a pastry bag with a tip, put leftover 3/4 cup whipped topping. Decoratively pipe topping on pie. Drizzle caramel and chocolate syrups on top. Sprinkle chopped peanut butter cups on top.

## Nutrition Information

- Calories: 649 calories;
- Total Carbohydrate: 56.7 g

- Cholesterol: 37 mg

- Total Fat: 44 g

- Protein: 12.9 g

- Sodium: 413 mg

# No Bake Peanut Butter Pie

Serving: 16 | Prep: 20m | Ready in: 2h20m

## Ingredients

• 1 (8 ounce) package cream cheese

• 1 1/2 cups confectioners' sugar

• 1 cup peanut butter

• 1 cup milk

• 1 (16 ounce) package frozen whipped topping, thawed

• 2 (9 inch) prepared graham cracker crusts

## Direction

• Blend together confectioners' sugar and cream cheese. Stir in milk and peanut butter. Blend until smooth. Fold in whipped topping.
• Scoop into 2 9 inches graham cracker pie shells; wrap it up, let it freeze in the freezer until set.

## Nutrition Information

- Calories: 432 calories;
- Total Carbohydrate: 41.4 g

- Cholesterol: 17 mg

- Total Fat: 27.8 g

- Protein: 7.2 g

- Sodium: 299 mg

# Peanut Buttery Chocolate Pie

Serving: 8

## Ingredients

- 1 cup peanut butter
- 2 cups confectioners' sugar
- 1 cup all-purpose flour
- 1/2 cup packed brown sugar
- 2/3 cup honey
- 1 tablespoon vanilla extract
- 1 cup semi-sweet chocolate chips
- 1/2 cup peanut butter chips
- 1 (9 inch) prepared graham cracker crust

## Direction

- In a mixing bowl, mix together confectioners' sugar, vanilla extract, honey and peanut butter. Use an electric mixer to mix thoroughly. Mix brown sugar and flour together then fold into the peanut butter mixture. Then fold peanut butter chips into the pie filling.

• Put chocolate chips in a microwave-safe bowl then microwave chocolate chips until they are melted. Stir the chocolate once in a while until it is smooth. Spread chocolate uniformly on the bottom of the graham cracker crust. Transfer the pie filling to the crust, spread the filling evenly. Let the pie chill then serve.

## Nutrition Information

• Calories: 845 calories;
• Total Carbohydrate: 125.6 g

• Cholesterol: 0 mg

• Total Fat: 34.2 g

• Protein: 15.8 g

• Sodium: 362 mg

# Reese Cup Pie I

Serving: 8 | Prep: 15m | Ready in: 4h15m

## Ingredients

- 1 (9 inch) pie shell, baked
- 3/4 cup peanut butter

- 2 1/4 cups cold milk

- 1 (5.9 ounce) package instant chocolate pudding mix

## Direction

- Use a mixer on low speed to cream peanut butter in a medium mixing bowl until soft. Slowly add milk while continuing mixing. (This is very important; if milk is added too fast, peanut butter will become hard.)
- When the peanut butter and all milk are well combined, put in pudding mix and continue beating until all ingredients are well incorporated and smooth, about 1 1/2 minutes.

• Put mixture into baked pie crust. Refrigerate for at least 4 hours before serving.

**Nutrition Information**

• Calories: 336 calories;
• Total Carbohydrate: 33.9 g

• Cholesterol: 5 mg

• Total Fat: 19.1 g

• Protein: 9.5 g

• Sodium: 536 mg

# Ryan's Peanut Butter Protein Pie

Serving: 8 | Prep: 10m | Ready in: 10h10m

## Ingredients

• 4 (4 ounce) packages single serve ready-made, fat free, chocolate pudding

• 1/2 cup reduced-fat creamy peanut butter

• 2 scoops chocolate-flavored protein powder

• 1 (8 ounce) container lite frozen whipped topping

• 1 (9 inch) prepared graham cracker crust

## Direction

• In a bowl, stir pudding and peanut butter together until smooth; put in protein powder and mix. Fold in whipped topping until the filling is mixed.

• Put filling into the prepped pie crust. Rest in the freezer 8 hours to overnight until set. Defrost in the fridge for 2 hours before serving.

## Nutrition Information

- Calories: 374 calories;
- Total Carbohydrate: 47.6 g

- Cholesterol: 1 mg

- Total Fat: 16.7 g

- Protein: 11.3 g

- Sodium: 406 mg

# Smooth And Creamy Peanut Butter Pie

Serving: 8 | Prep: 15m | Ready in: 3h15m

## Ingredients

- 3/4 cup creamy peanut butter
- 1 (3 ounce) package cream cheese
- 1 1/4 cups confectioners' sugar
- 1 (12 ounce) container frozen whipped topping, thawed
- 1 (9 inch) prepared chocolate cookie crumb crust

## Direction

- Combine sugar, cream cheese and peanut butter in a large bowl. Then mix whipped topping into the peanut butter mixture. Whisk until smooth and there's no lump left.
- Put filling mixture into pie crust and let the pie firm up in the fridge for about 3 hours.

**Nutrition Information**

- Calories: 527 calories;
- Total Carbohydrate: 48.5 g

- Cholesterol: 12 mg

- Total Fat: 35.2 g

- Protein: 8.8 g

- Sodium: 340 mg

# NO-BAKE PIE RECIPES

# Chocolate Banana Cream Pie

Serving: 8

## Ingredients

- 1 (9 inch) deep dish pie crust, baked and cooled
- 2 (1 ounce) squares semisweet chocolate
- 1 tablespoon milk
- 1 tablespoon butter
- 2 bananas, sliced
- 1 1/2 cups cold milk
- 1 (3.5 ounce) package instant vanilla pudding mix
- 1 1/2 cups shredded coconut
- 1 1/2 cups frozen whipped topping, thawed
- 2 tablespoons flaked coconut, toasted

## Direction

• In a medium, microwaveable bowl, mix butter or margarine, 1 tablespoon milk, and chocolate. Turn the microwave on high for 1 to 1 1/2 minutes, mixing every 30 seconds. Mix until chocolate is melted completely. Put in pie crust evenly.

• Put banana slices on top of chocolate.

• Into a large bowl, put 1 1/2 cups milk. Put pudding mix and whisk for 2 minutes with wire whisk. Mix in 1 1/2 cups coconut. Scoop on top of banana slices in crust.

• Put whipped topping evenly over pie. Scatter with toasted coconut. Chill 4 hours, or until firm. Store in the fridge.

## Nutrition Information

• Calories: 373 calories;
• Total Carbohydrate: 46.7 g

• Cholesterol: 8 mg

• Total Fat: 20 g

• Protein: 4.1 g

• Sodium: 400 mg

# Chocolate Bar Pie I

Serving: 8

## Ingredients

- 1 (9 inch) prepared graham cracker crust
- 6 (1.45 ounce) bars milk chocolate with almonds candy

- 18 large marshmallows

- 1/2 cup milk

- 1 cup heavy whipping cream

- 1 teaspoon vanilla extract

## Direction

• Break chocolate almond bars into pieces and put in a medium saucepan with milk and marshmallows. Put over medium-high heat and stir regularly to melt the marshmallows and chocolate and until smooth. Take away from heat and let cool.

• Whip cream in a medium bowl until soft peaks form. Fold the cream into the cooled chocolate mixture. Stir vanilla extract in gently. Put mixture into pie shell. Refrigerate before serving.

## Nutrition Information

• Calories: 473 calories;

• Total Carbohydrate: 50.7 g

• Cholesterol: 48 mg

• Total Fat: 29.4 g

• Protein: 5.4 g

• Sodium: 224 mg

# Chocolate Bar Pie Ii

Serving: 8

## Ingredients

• 1 (9 inch) prepared graham cracker crust

• 6 (1.45 ounce) bars milk chocolate with almonds, coarsely chopped

• 2 cups miniature marshmallows

• 1/2 cup milk

• 1 pinch salt

• 1 cup heavy whipping cream

## Direction

• Put salt, milk, marshmallows, and chopped chocolate bars in the top of a double boiler. Put the boiler on heat then stir till the mixture is melted and becomes smooth. Get the boiler off heat and let it cool, remember to stir once in a while.

• Beat cream till there are soft peaks in a medium bowl. Fold cream into the cooled chocolate mixture. Transfer the mixture into graham cracker crust. Keep it chill before serving. The pie also tastes great when you serve it frozen.

## Nutrition Information

• Calories: 459 calories;
• Total Carbohydrate: 47.6 g

• Cholesterol: 48 mg

• Total Fat: 29.3 g

• Protein: 5.4 g

• Sodium: 221 mg

# Chocolate Chiffon Pie

Serving: 8 | Prep: 25m | Ready in: 2h25m

## Ingredients

- 1 (9 inch) pie crust, baked

- 1/4 cup cold water

- 1 envelope (1 tablespoon) unflavored gelatin

- 2 (1 ounce) squares unsweetened chocolate, grated

- 1/2 cup boiling water

- 4 egg yolks

- 1/2 cup white sugar

- 1/4 teaspoon salt

- 1 teaspoon vanilla extract

- 4 egg whites

- 1/2 cup white sugar

## Direction

• In a small bowl, put cold water and scatter gelatin on top. Put aside for 5 minutes to soften. In a large heatproof bowl, put grated chocolate. Pour boiling water on chocolate and mix until smooth. Mix gelatin mixture into chocolate blend; mix to dissolve gelatin completely.

• Beat half cup sugar with egg yolks in a small bowl until light and smooth. Whip egg yolks into chocolate blend, then mix in vanilla extract and salt. Let rest to cool.

• Whip egg whites in a large glass or metal mixing bowl until foamy. Put remaining 1/2 cup sugar slowly, keep whisking until white forms stiff peaks. Into cooled chocolate mixture, fold egg whites. Put into baked pastry shell and refrigerate for at least 2 hours, or until set.

## Nutrition Information

• Calories: 252 calories;

• Total Carbohydrate: 35.4 g

• Cholesterol: 102 mg

• Total Fat: 11 g

• Protein: 5.5 g

• Sodium: 210 mg

# Chocolate Cream Pie I

Serving: 8

## Ingredients

- 3/4 cup white sugar
- 1/3 cup all-purpose flour
- 2 cups milk
- 2 (1 ounce) squares unsweetened chocolate
- 3 egg yolks
- 2 tablespoons butter
- 1 teaspoon vanilla extract
- 1 (9 inch) pie shell, baked

## Direction

- In a 2 quarts saucepan, mix chopped up chocolate, milk, flour and sugar. Mixing continuously, cook over medium heat until mixture starts to bubble. Keep mixing for 2 minutes.

• Stir a little hot mixture into the egg yolks, blending quickly to avoid the yolks from being cooked. Mix the warm egg yolk mixture into the remaining chocolate mixture and cook for 90 seconds more. Take away from heat and mix in vanilla and butter or margarine.

• Put filling into pie crust, refrigerate until firm. Spread whipped topping and some grated chocolate on top.

## Nutrition Information

• Calories: 322 calories;
• Total Carbohydrate: 38.6 g

• Cholesterol: 89 mg

• Total Fat: 17.2 g

• Protein: 5.9 g

• Sodium: 172 mg

# Chocolate Cream Pie Ii

Serving: 8

## Ingredients

- 1 (9 inch) pie crust, baked
- 3 egg yolks, beaten
- 1 1/2 cups white sugar
- 3 tablespoons cornstarch
- 1/2 cup unsweetened cocoa powder
- 1/2 teaspoon salt
- 3 cups milk
- 1 tablespoon butter
- 1 1/2 teaspoons vanilla extract
- 1 cup frozen whipped topping, thawed

## Direction

• Put sugar and egg yolks in a large mixing bowl then cream together. Stir in salt, cocoa powder and cornstarch. Pour in milk and stir gently.

• Transfer mixture to a large saucepan then cook over medium heat, remember to stir continuously till the mixture boils. Get the saucepan away from heat. Add vanilla extract and margarine or butter and stir. Let cool slightly, pour the cooled mixture into pastry shell. Allow the mixture to chill till ready to serve. Use whipped topping to garnish.

## Nutrition Information

• Calories: 360 calories;
• Total Carbohydrate: 57.7 g

• Cholesterol: 88 mg

• Total Fat: 13.2 g

• Protein: 5.9 g

• Sodium: 302 mg

# Chocolate Hazelnut Mocha Cappuccino Pie

Serving: 8 | Prep: 10m | Ready in: 2h10m

## Ingredients

- 1 (3.4 ounce) package instant vanilla pudding mix
- 1 1/2 cups cold milk
- 2 tablespoons instant mocha cappuccino mix
- 2 cups frozen whipped topping, thawed
- 1 (9 inch) prepared chocolate cookie crumb crust
- 1/2 cup semisweet chocolate chips
- 1/2 cup chopped hazelnuts

## Direction

• Cook pudding following package directions with the coffee mix and milk. Fold into pudding half a cup whipped topping, then put mixture into pie crust and spread out. Scatter a quarter cup chocolate chips and a quarter cup of hazelnuts on top of pie. Wrap it up and chill in the fridge for 2 hours.

• Put 1 1/2 cups of remaining whipped topping on pie, then garnish with remaining hazelnuts and chocolate chips.

## Nutrition Information

• Calories: 377 calories;
• Total Carbohydrate: 39.7 g

• Cholesterol: 5 mg

• Total Fat: 23.2 g

• Protein: 5.9 g

• Sodium: 278 mg

# Creamy Avocado Pie

Serving: 8 | Prep: 15m | Ready in: 4h15m

## Ingredients

- 2 avocados - halved, peeled, and pitted
- 1 (14 ounce) can sweetened condensed milk
- 1 (8 ounce) package cream cheese
- 1/3 cup lemon juice
- 1 teaspoon vanilla extract
- 1 (9 inch) graham cracker crust
- 1 (8 ounce) container sour cream
- 1 tablespoon white sugar
- 1 teaspoon vanilla extract

## Direction

• Blend 1 tsp. vanilla extract, lemon juice, cream cheese, sweetened condensed milk and avocados till smooth in blender; put in graham cracker crust.

• Mix vanilla extract, sugar and sour cream in bowl; put on avocado filling. Refrigerate pie for 4 hours till set.

## Nutrition Information

• Calories: 555 calories;
• Total Carbohydrate: 55 g

• Cholesterol: 60 mg

• Total Fat: 34.8 g

• Protein: 9.2 g

• Sodium: 334 mg

# Creamy Chocolate Mousse Pie

Serving: 10 | Prep: 20m | Ready in: 3h30m

## Ingredients

• 1 1/2 cups miniature marshmallows

• 1 (7 ounce) bar milk chocolate candy

• 1/2 cup milk

• 2 cups heavy whipping cream

• 1 (9 inch) pie shell, baked

## Direction

• Put milk, chocolate candy, marshmallows in a saucepan, heat over low heat until chocolate and marshmallows are melted, remember to stir continuously. Let mixture cool completely.

• In a large bowl, beat heavy cream till forming stiff peaks. Life your whisk or beater straight up: there will be sharp peaks formed by the whipped cream. Fold cooled chocolate mixture gently in whipped cream till everything combines well, transfer the mixture to baked pie shell. Keep in the fridge for about 3 hours until set.

## Nutrition Information

- Calories: 399 calories;
- Total Carbohydrate: 29.1 g
- Cholesterol: 71 mg
- Total Fat: 30.5 g
- Protein: 3.5 g
- Sodium: 142 mg

# Creamy Lemon Pie Ii

Serving: 8 | Prep: 30m | Ready in: 30m

## Ingredients

- 1/2 cup water

- 1 1/2 teaspoons unflavored gelatin

- 1 lemon, juiced

- 1 2/3 cups frozen whipped topping, thawed

- 1 (9 inch) pie shell, baked

## Direction

• Mix gelatin and water in a small microwave safe bowl. Then microwave for 1 minute. Stir the lemon juice in. To lighten up, fold 1/3 of the whipped topping in, then fold in the reserved whipped topping until there are no streaks left. Pour mixture into baked pie crust. Refrigerate until ready to serve.

**Nutrition Information**

- Calories: 172 calories;
- Total Carbohydrate: 15.7 g

- Cholesterol: 0 mg

- Total Fat: 11.8 g

- Protein: 2.2 g

- Sodium: 127 mg

# French Silk Chocolate Pie I

Serving: 8 | Prep: 20m | Ready in: 2h20m

## Ingredients

• 1/2 cup butter, room temperature

• 3/4 cup white sugar

• 2 (1 ounce) squares unsweetened baking chocolate, melted and cooled

• 1 teaspoon vanilla extract

• 2 eggs

• 1 prepared 8 inch pastry shell, baked and cooled

## Direction

• In a mixing bowl, cream the butter. Use an electric mixer to gradually beat in the sugar until the butter becomes pale and well mixed. Mix in the vanilla extract and the completely cooled chocolate. Add the eggs, one by one, beating for 5 minutes on medium speed with each time you add the egg. Scoop the chocolate filling into a baked and chilled pie crust.

• Rest in the fridge for at least 2 hours before serving.

## Nutrition Information

• Calories: 294 calories;
• Total Carbohydrate: 27.3 g

• Cholesterol: 77 mg

• Total Fat: 20.6 g

• Protein: 3.2 g

• Sodium: 183 mg

# Fresh Berry Pie

Serving: 8

## Ingredients

- 4 (3 ounce) packages strawberry flavored Jell-O®
- 4 tablespoons cornstarch

- 1 cup white sugar

- 1 cup boiling water

- 1 quart fresh strawberries, hulled

- 1 (9 inch) prepared graham cracker crust

## Direction

- Mix boiling water, sugar, gelatin power and cornstarch in a large saucepan. Cook with medium-high heat, frequently stir until the mixture boils and thickens. Let it cool down to room temperature while preparing the berries.

• To the cooled gelatin mixture, add in the berries. Mix gently to coat, then pour everything into the crust. Chill for 1 hour uncovered, then cover and refrigerate.

**Nutrition Information**

• Calories: 419 calories;
• Total Carbohydrate: 87.9 g

• Cholesterol: 0 mg

• Total Fat: 6.8 g

• Protein: 5.4 g

• Sodium: 323 mg

# Fresh Fruit Custard Tart

Serving: 8 | Prep: 30m | Ready in: 3h

## Ingredients

• 1 (9 inch) refrigerated pie crust

• 1 cup Egg Beaters® Original

• 1/2 cup granulated sugar

• 1 teaspoon vanilla extract

• 2 cups fat free milk

• 2 cups assorted fresh fruit (such as blueberries, sliced strawberries, and/or peaches)

• Reddi-wip Original Whipped Light Cream

## Direction

• Heat oven to 350°F to preheat. Put pie crust in 9-in. pie dish, firmly press the crust into sides and bottom of plate. Flute the edge.

• In a large bowl with wire whisk, whip vanilla, sugar and Egg Beaters until combined. Slowly whisk in milk until blended. Put pastry shell in heated oven. Gently put filling into prepped pastry. Bake until a knife inserted near center comes out clean, or 40 minutes. Let it cool totally on a wire rack.

• Let it rest in the fridge about 2 hours until set. Put fruit on top.

• Slice pie into 8 pieces. Decorate slices with a serving of Reddi-wip just before serving (optional).

## Nutrition Information

• Calories: 234 calories;
• Total Carbohydrate: 32 g

• Cholesterol: 4 mg

• Total Fat: 8.2 g

• Protein: 7.4 g

• Sodium: 204 mg

# Fresh Mango Pie Dessert

Serving: 24 | Prep: 15m | Ready in: 2h20m

## Ingredients

• 2 cups all-purpose flour, sifted

• 1/2 cup confectioners' sugar

• 3/4 cup butter

• 1 (8 ounce) package cream cheese, softened

• 1/2 cup white sugar

• 1 teaspoon vanilla extract

• 3/4 (12 ounce) container whipped topping (such as Cool Whip®)

• 1 cup cold water

• 2 envelopes unflavored gelatin

• 1 cup boiling water

• 1/2 cup white sugar, or to taste

• 1/4 teaspoon salt

- 1/4 cup lemon juice

- 5 cups diced mango

## Direction

- Set oven to 350°F (175°C) to preheat.
- In a bowl, combine confectioners' sugar and flour together. With a pastry blender or 2 pastry knives, slice butter into flour mixture until mixture forms coarse crumbs; push into a 9x13-inch baking dish.

- Bake for 20 to 25 minutes in the preheated oven until crust is slightly browned. Take off from oven and let it rest to cool completely.

- With an electric mixer, blend vanilla extract, 1/2 cup white sugar and cream cheese together in a bowl until creamy and smooth. Into cream cheese mixture, fold whipped topping and put on the crust. Chill mixture for about 30 minutes until cream cheese filling is cold.

- Put cold water into a bowl and dust with gelatin; mix well. Put hot water on the gelatin mixture and mix to dissolve the gelatin. Combine salt and 1/2 cup sugar into gelatin mixture until sugar is dissolved; pour lemon juice and bring it to room temperature. Into gelatin mixture, fold mango and chill for 15 to 20 minutes until gelatin begin to firm up.

• Put mango gelatin on the cream cheese filling and chill for about 1 hour until completely firm.

## Nutrition Information

• Calories: 219 calories;
• Total Carbohydrate: 27.1 g

• Cholesterol: 26 mg

• Total Fat: 11.7 g

• Protein: 2.5 g

• Sodium: 101 mg

# THANK YOU

Thank you for choosing *Cooking Methods for Beginners: No-Bake Desserts* for improving your cooking skills! I hope you enjoyed making the recipes as much as tasting them! If you're interested in learning new recipes and new meals to cook, go and check out the other books of the series.

CPSIA information can be obtained
at www.ICGtesting.com
Printed in the USA
LVHW010755160621
690358LV00016B/3506